D0119058

ASSASSIN'S CREED™

3 | ACCIPITER

STORY : CORBEYRAN
ART : DJILLALI DEFALI
COLOR : ALEXIS SENTENAC

ASSASSIN'S CREED: ACCIPITER

ISBN: 9781781163429

Published by Titan Books
A division of Titan Publishing Group Ltd.
144 Southwark St.
London
SE1 0UP

First Titan edition: October 2012
English-language translation: Mark McKenzie-Ray

A CIP catalogue record for this title is available from the British Library

10 9 8 7 6 5 4 3 2

Printed in the United States of America

ACKNOWLEDGMENTS

Thank you to Djillali Defali for setting me on this fascinating adventure. To Alexis Nolent for being my guide and accompanying me through this new territory. Thanks also to François Tallec, Olivier Henriot and Geoffroy Sardi, as well as the teams at Ubisoft Paris and Montreal, for opening their doors and welcoming me into this universe.

CORBEYRAN

Thank you to Matz for the phone call, even if you regretted it afterwards, I didn't let you down, buddy! Thanks to the whole team at Ubisoft Montreal for their time and patience. Benjamin Dennel – thank you, my friend, for the motivation and encouragement. And a huge thanks to François Tallec, for supporting me during the creation of the album – I know it wasn't easy!

DEFALI

Thank you to Yves Guillemot, Alain Corre, Serge Hascoet, Jade Raymond, Patrice Desilets, Corey May, Sébastien Puel, Mohamed Gambouz, Olivier Henriot, Mathieu Ferland, Audrey-Ann Milot, Tommy Francois, Thomas Paincon, Florent Greffe and Marie-Anne Boutet.
Thanks also to Vladimir Lentzy, Philippe Hédouin, Frédéric Noaro and the rest of the team at Dargaud for their support.

LES DEUX ROYAUMES

[1] THE RHONE RIVER.
[2] GENEVA, WHICH TODAY CAN BE FOUND IN SWITZERLAND.
[3] A LARGE, DEFENDED, IRON AGE SETTLEMENT.

ALLOW ME TO CONGRATULATE YOU ON ANOTHER VICTORY, ACCIPITER!
WOULD THAT YOU TELL ME YOUR NAME, STRANGER, AND I SHALL THANK YOU IN RETURN.
YOU HAVE FORGOTTEN MY VOICE AND ACCENT?! I PRAY THAT YOU HAVE NOT ALSO FORGOTTEN MY FACE!
CUERVO OF IBERIA!
I DID NOT EXPECT TO SEE YOU SO EARLY IN MY JOURNEY, DEAR FRIEND!
YOUR JOURNEY IS EXACTLY THE REASON FOR MY VISIT.
MY JOURNEY?
YES, SPECIFICALLY YOUR NEXT STOP TOWARDS THE SOUTH, LUGDUNUM!
THE GAUL CAPITAL IS A POWERFUL CITY. I WILL NOT DISGUISE THE FACT THAT MY MEN WOULD PREFER TO AVOID IT RATHER THAN FIGHT-- BUT, PERSONALLY, I REMAIN CONFIDENT THAT WE CAN VANQUISH ITS FORCES!
YOUR REPUTATION PRECEDES YOU, ACCIPITER, LIKE THE SCENT OF A GREAT FEAST CARRIED ALONG BY THE NIGHT AIR. BUT IT ALSO YIELDS ANXIETY WITHIN OUR CIRCLE.
I'M LISTENING...

'AN OLD LATIN WORD THAT THE ASSASSINS APPLIED TO THOSE WHO WERE PART OF THEIR ORDER. 'CIRCULUM' MEANS CIRCLE. 'LIBERALIS' IS A NOTION WHICH PERTAINS TO FREE, HONORABLE, AND LIBERAL MEN.

ROME, THE NEXT DAY.
IF MY MEMORY SERVES, THIS VILLA BELONGS TO SENATOR VULTUR.
THAT MONGREL WILL REGRET HIS ACTIONS!
THAT MAN, WHO PLUNGED HIS DAGGER INTO THE HEART OF MY FATHER, WILL SEE THE SUN SET FOR THE VERY LAST TIME TODAY.

5

?!
HELP! HEEEEEELP!
AARGH
6

EUGH!
NOOOOO!
TINKK!
AAAAH!
NOW. YOU WILL TAKE ME TO YOUR MASTER'S LODGINGS IF YOU WISH TO KEEP YOUR LIFE.
I... I... OKAY...

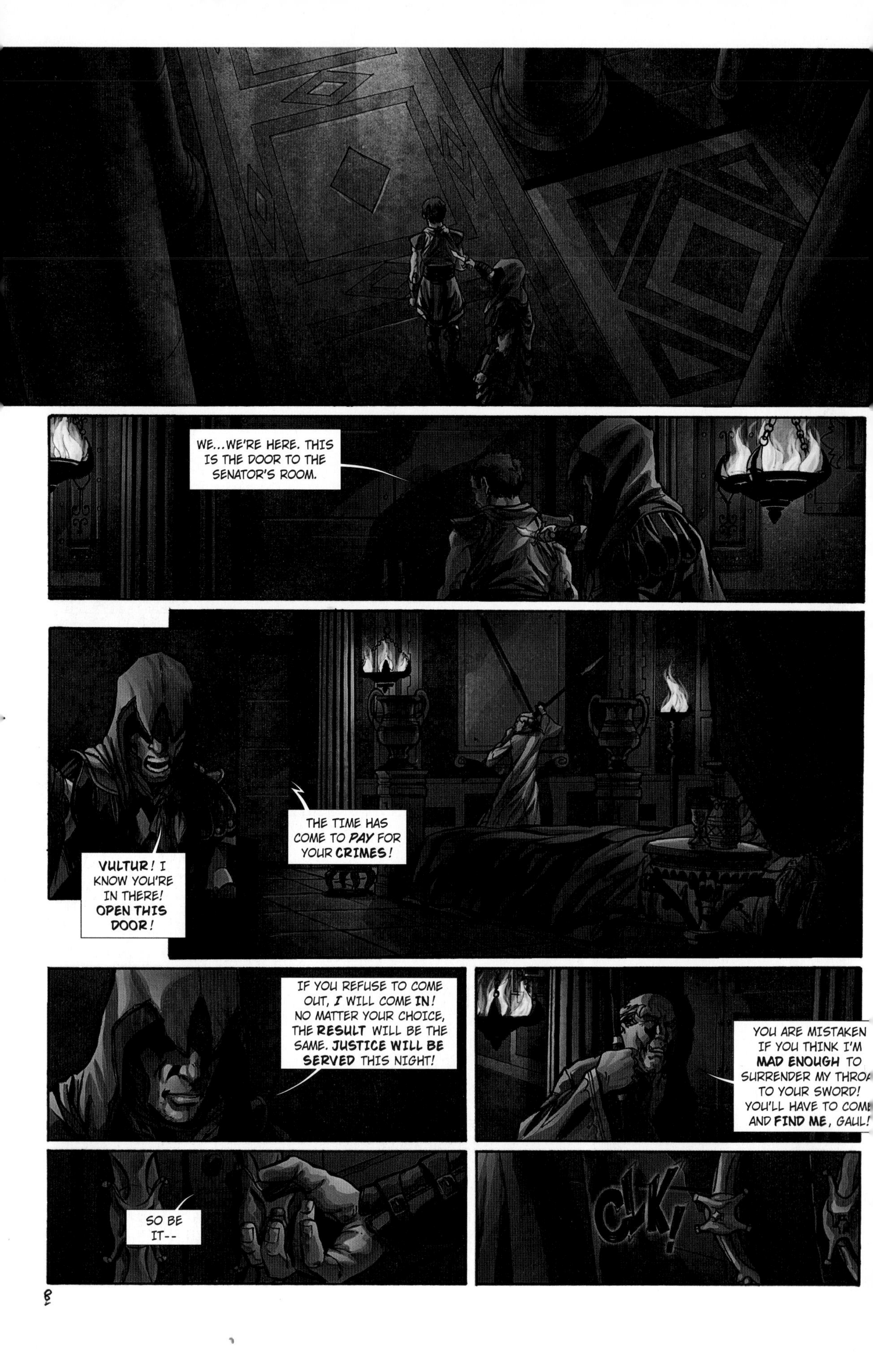
WE...WE'RE HERE. THIS IS THE DOOR TO THE SENATOR'S ROOM.
VULTUR! I KNOW YOU'RE IN THERE! OPEN THIS DOOR!
THE TIME HAS COME TO PAY FOR YOUR CRIMES!
IF YOU REFUSE TO COME OUT, I WILL COME IN! NO MATTER YOUR CHOICE, THE RESULT WILL BE THE SAME. JUSTICE WILL BE SERVED THIS NIGHT!
YOU ARE MISTAKEN IF YOU THINK I'M MAD ENOUGH TO SURRENDER MY THROA TO YOUR SWORD! YOU'LL HAVE TO COME AND FIND ME, GAUL!
SO BE IT--
CLK!

DIE, YOU SON OF A BITCH!
TCCHKKK!
AAAAH!
NICE TRY, VULTUR! ALAS, THERE GOES YOUR ONLY MEANS OF DEFENCE.
SCRRAAAA!
IT'S TIME TO FINISH THIS!
COMMEND YOUR SPIRIT TO THE GODS, YOU SNAKE!
SPARE ME, AQUILUS, AND I WILL MAKE YOU A RICH MAN!
I SCOFF AT YOUR RICHES. THE FIGHT THAT I'M LEADING IS FAR MORE IMPORTANT!
YOU ARE FANATICAL! A...A MADMAN--LIKE YOUR FATHER! YOU THINK YOURSELF BETTER THAN ME? PISH!
YOU ASSASSINATED MY FATHER! AS HIS SON, IT IS MY DUTY TO AVENGE THIS ODIOUS CRIME!
NO--!
H...HAVE MERCY--
MERCY? DID YOU SHOW THE SMALLEST SCRAP OF MERCY FOR LUCIUS AS YOU KILLED HIM?

BE UNDER NO ILLUSION, VULTUR. YOU WILL DIE. BUT BEFORE I KILL YOU, YOU ARE GOING TO REVEAL THE LOCATION OF THE ANKH THAT YOU STOLE.
IT IS IN THE CHEST. THERE!
GIVE IT TO ME!
ALL IN GOOD TIME, AQUILUS! DO YOU KNOW THE ORIGIN OF THIS OBJECT? OR JUST HOW VALUABLE IT REALLY IS?
I AM AWARE OF ITS PURPOSE. UNFORTUNATELY, MY FATHER DIED BEFORE HE COULD DISCLOSE ANY FURTHER DETAILS...
ACCORDING TO LEGEND, THE ANKH BELONGED TO ISIS...
THE MOTHER GODDESS WAS WORSHIPPED ACROSS THE ENTIRE NILE DELTA.
"THANKS TO THIS MAGICAL CROSS, ISIS PROTECTED THE EGYPTIAN KINGS FROM DECAYING...
10

"THE LEGEND TELLS US THAT WHEN OSIRIS DIED, ISIS WAS COMPLETELY DISTRAUGHT FROM GRIEF AND HEARTACHE...
"THE GODDESS USED THE ANKH TO BRING HER HUSBAND BACK TO LIFE FOR A SINGLE NIGHT.
"FROM THEIR CARNAL UNION, HORUS WAS BORN.
"IT WAS FROM THIS MOMENT THAT THE POWERS OF REGENERATION AND COMMUNICATION WITH BEINGS FROM BEYOND WERE ATTRIBUTED TO THIS ANSATE CROSS.
"MORE THAN 200 YEARS AGO, THE ANKH WAS COVERED FROM A PYRAMID BY ROMAN LOOTERS.
"IT WAS SOLD TO A SLAVE TRADER FOR NEXT TO NOTHING, WHO BROUGHT IT WITH HIM, RIGHT HERE TO ROME, WHERE E RETIRED. BANKRUPT AND IGNORANT OF ITS REAL VALUE, HE GOT RID OF THE OBJECT AT A VERY LOW PRICE.
"THE CROSS THEN PASSED FROM HAND TO HAND. IT WAS SOLD AND RESOLD ON MANY OCCASIONS AND FELL INTO OBLIVION AFTER BEING LOST."

RECENTLY, THE ANKH WAS REDISCOVERED IN GERMANIA AND RECOVERED BY YOUR COUSIN, ACCIPITER, THE ALEMANNI, WHO HAD HEARD OF THE FORMIDABLE POWER THAT HAD BEEN ACCREDITED TO THE MYTHICAL OBJECT.
AND IT WAS ACCIPITER WHO PUT IT INTO MY HANDS. NOW--ENOUGH! GIVE IT TO ME!

I WOULD RATHER DIE!
?!

"HOW'S IT GOING, REBECCA
"PERFECTLY WELL, LUCY. THANKS."

MONTERIGGIONI VILLA, ITALY. TODAY.
DESMOND'S GENETIC MEMORY IS LIMITLESS!
EVERY DETAIL IS RECORDED WITH INFINITE PRECISION.
YES, IT'S ABSOLUTELY INCREDIBLE!
HMMM. WHAT IS IT EXACTLY YOU FIND INCREDIBLE, LUCY? THE SUBJECT-- OR HIS MEMORY?
WHAT ARE YOU TRYING TO INSINUATE, REBECCA? THAT I'M TOO CLOSE TO DESMOND? AM I BEING UNPROFESSIONAL?
BELIEVE ME, LUCY, JUST BECAUSE I'M HERE TO OPERATE THE ANIMUS, DOESN'T MEAN THAT I'VE NEVER NOTICED IT.
I, MYSELF, WOULDN'T DREAM OF DOING IT! BUT SO LONG AS YOU DO THE WORK, TO THE BEST OF YOUR ABILITY, YOU SHOULDN'T HAVE TO NEGLECT YOUR FEELINGS.
YOUR COMMENTS ARE COMPLETELY OUT OF LINE, REBECCA! THERE IS NOTHING GOING ON!
OKAY, OKAY. I'M SORRY. I DIDN'T KNOW IT WAS SUCH A DELICATE SUBJECT.
LET'S JUST DROP IT. WE HAVE TO STAY FOCUSED.
"AQUILUS IS WHAT'S IMPORTANT RIGHT NOW. NOTHING ELSE MATTERS."
13

AQUILUS! PRAISE BE TO THE GODS! YOU ARE ALIVE!
VALERIA, AFTER ALL THIS TIME...

I AM SO HAPPY TO SEE YOU AGAIN!

I WANTED TO BE PRESENT AT YOUR FATHER'S FUNERAL, BUT REGRETTABLY, I RECEIVED YOUR MESSAGE TOO LATE.
LUCIUS WAS BURIED AT HIS OWN HOME ACCORDING TO THE SACRED RITES. TODAY, HIS SOUL RESTS AMONGST THOSE OF OTHER HEROES AND WISE MEN.

HIS HONOR HAS BEEN... AVENGED.

BY MY HAND, THE BLOOD OF HIS ASSASSIN RUNS.

AND I HAVE RECLAIMED THE OBJECT THAT HE STOLE FROM MY FATHER.
WAS IT FOR THIS OBJECT THAT YOU HAD TO LEAVE YOUR WIFE AND DESERT YOUR HOME FOR SO LONG?
MY LIFE IS WORTH LESS THAN THE MISSION THAT WAS ENTRUSTED TO ME.

WILL THERE EVER BE AN END TO THESE HORRORS?!
NOT AS LONG AS WAR AND HATRED STIR THE HEARTS OF MEN!
AND WHAT OF LOVE?
WHAT YOU OFFER ME IS WORTHY OF A KING.
I LOVE YOU, VALERIA!

15

TK TK
DESMOND?
CAN YOU HEAR ME, DESMOND?
WH...WHAT'S HAPPENING?
I'VE DISCONNECTED THE ANIMUS.
IS THERE A PROBLEM?
WE'VE GOT INTRUDERS TRESPASSING IN THE GROUNDS.
THE OTHERS HAVE GONE. ONLY US, REBECCA, AND SHAUN ARE LEFT. BUT **THEY** AREN'T TRAINED FOR **COMBAT**.
THERE'S NO NEED FOR SUCH CONCERN. I'M READY.
ARE YOU **SURE**?
ARE YOU WORRIED ABOUT ME, LUCY?
WORRIED? NO, NOT REALLY. I JUST DON'T WANT OUR GREATEST AND MOST SUCCESSFUL SUBJECT GETTING INJURED AT SUCH A PIVOTAL MOMENT.

SCHOCK!
AARGH
SCHOCK!
EUGH!
TWK!
EUGH!
SCHOCK!
SCHOCK!
OW!

PAW!
PWW!
GGHHH!
I THOUGHT I HAD THEM THIS TIME!
ARE YOU HURT?
URGH, NO. I TOOK A NASTY BLOW, BUT NOTHING FATAL. IF YOU HADN'T INTERVENED--
WE CAN CONGRATULATE OURSELVES LATER. ARE YOU SURE YOU'RE OKAY?
YEAH. YOU'RE NOT WORRIED ABOUT ME, ARE YOU, DESMOND?
SURE! WHY WOULDN'T I BE? WE'RE NOT ALL AS COLD-HEARTED AS YOU, ICE QUEEN--
I DARE YOU TO SAY THAT AGAIN!!

PLEASE, DESMOND.... STOP.
IS SOMETHING WRONG?
NO. IT'S JUST--I DON'T KNOW IF THAT WAS SUCH A GOOD IDEA...
SORRY, LUCY. I DIDN'T MEAN TO **EMBARRASS** YOU.
YOU DON'T HAVE TO BE **SORRY**, DESMOND. IT'S JUST THAT...
WE'RE **ASSASSINS**, YOU AND I. WE HAVE A MISSION TO COMPLETE, IMPORTANT INFORMATION TO COLLECT. AND IT'S **NEVER** A GOOD IDEA TO LET FEELINGS GET IN THE WAY.
I GUESS. I MEAN--YEAH, YOU'RE PROBABLY RIGHT.
SO, WHO DO YOU THINK THESE MEN WERE? TEMPLARS?
COULD BE...
AND **THIS**? HAVE YOU SEEN IT BEFORE?
YEAH, I NOTICED IT WHEN WE ARRIVED.
WHAT IS IT?
I DON'T KNOW ANYTHING ABOUT IT...
NO DOUBT AN ALTAR CONSECRATED TO ONE OF THE **OWNERS** OF THIS VILLA.
20

DO YOU THINK HE'S HAD LONG ENOUGH TO REST?
HMMM. **MENTALLY**, HE SHOULD BE ABLE TO HANDLE IT.
BUT I'VE INJECTED HIM WITH A DOSE OF **ATROPINE** SO HIS HEART CAN WITHSTAND THE PRESSURE WE'RE PUTTING ON IT.

"WHERE IS HE?"
"STILL IN 279AD... SOMEWHERE ON THE UPLAND WHICH OVERLOOKS LUGDUNUM, THE GAULISH CAPITAL..."

PEACE **HAS** NO PRICE, PREFECT!

YOU SHOULD BE **ELATED** AT THE CONDITIONS I'M OFFERING YOU, TO SPARE YOUR CITY.

IF I UNDERSTAND YOU CORRECTLY, **BARBARIAN**, PEACE DOES **INDEED** HAVE A PRICE. AND IT IS AN EXTORTIONATE ONE!

HOLD BACK YOUR FLEA-RIDDEN HORDES...
AS YOU WISH. OUR TROOPS ARE BUT A STONE'S THROW AWAY. I CAN EASILY GIVE THE ORDER TO ATTACK!
HERE IS THE PAYMENT YOU DEMANDED.
YOU HAVE MADE A WISE DECISION, PREFECT.
TAKE ADVANTAGE OF THESE SMALL VICTORIES! ROME WILL ENSURE YOU MEET YOUR END-- SOONER OR LATER!
WE WILL SEE ABOUT THAT.
PREFECT, EVERYTHING IS IN PLACE FOR US TO ARREST AQUILUS.
?!
PERFECT!
EXECUTE HIM AND HIS WIFE WHEN THEY HAVE LEFT THE CITY... AND ENSURE THEIR BODIES ARE NEVER FOUND.

SHARE THE PAYMENT FROM THESE **COWARDS** BETWEEN YOURSELVES. DISTRIBUTE MY SHARE AMONGST THE MEN.
YOUR GENEROSITY WILL BE REWARDED ONE DAY, ACCIPITER!

ON THIS NIGHT, WE HAVE ANOTHER VICTORY TO CELEBRATE--AN **EASY** VICTORY! HAHAHA!

RETURN TO CAMP AND BEGIN YOUR CELEBRATIONS **WITHOUT** ME.

WHERE ARE YOU GOING?
TO LUGDUNUM.

HA HA! TO SULLY THE HONOR OF A WOMAN?

TO SAVE THE LIFE OF A MAN.

HOW'S IT GOING?
YEAH FINE... FALSE ALARM. NOTHING TO WORRY ABOUT.
AND YOU, SHAUN, ANYTHING NEW?
-:SIGH:- YOU KNOW FULL WELL NOTHING IS EVER NEW IN THE ARCHIVES!
I'M STILL RESEARCHING THE ANCIENT BRANCHES OF DESMOND'S FAMILY TREE...
AND I'VE FOUND TRACES OF ONE OF DESMOND'S ANCESTORS BY THE NAME OF LUGOS. ISN'T THAT STRANGE?
WHAT DO YOU MEAN, 'STRANGE'?
BECAUSE, IN LATIN, 'LUGOS' MEANS 'RAVEN'.
ANOTHER BRANCH OF COUSINS, LIKE ACCIPITER'S?
QUITE LIKELY. I'M GOING TO LOOK INTO IT RIGHT NOW.
GOOD LUCK, SHAUN. I'M GONNA HEAD BACK TO THE ANIMUS AND DIVE BACK INTO THE PAST-- NO HOLDS BARRED.
ARE YOU SURE YOU WANT TO GET BACK INTO THE ANIMUS STRAIGHT AWAY? IT MIGHT BE DANGEROUS.
IT'S MORE DANGEROUS BEING HERE! THE TEMPLARS SEEM TO HAVE SUCCESSFULLY LOCATED THIS VILLA.
WE'RE NOT SAFE HERE ANYMORE, LUCY. WE HAVE TO ACT QUICKLY AND GATHER AS MUCH DATA AS POSSIBLE BEFORE WE HAVE TO ESCAPE TO A NEW SITE.
OKAY, OKAY. YOU'RE RIGHT. LET'S GO!

OU STILL HAVEN'T REVEALED THE TRUE VALUE OF THIS OBJECT, AQUILUS.
I KNOW, VALERIA, I KNOW. I AM STILL STRUGGLING TO CONVINCE MYSELF WHAT IT REPRESENTS.
SURELY IT IS SIMPLY A CROSS?
BUT IT'S NO ORDINARY CROSS. THIS ANKH BELONGED TO THE GODDESS ISIS. IT'S THE SYMBOL OF ETERNITY.
THIS OBJECT IS A BRIDGE BETWEEN THE PAST AND THE PRESENT.
A LINE BETWEEN THE DEAD AND THE LIVING!
ARE YOU TELLING ME THAT, THANKS TO THIS OBJECT, DEAD BODIES ARE GOING TO COME ALIVE AND HAUNT US? THAT'S HORRIFYING!
NO, VALERIA, DO NOT WORRY. NO SPECTRE WILL SUDDENLY APPEAR BEFORE US!
I THOUGHT THAT FOR A MOMENT, TOO! BUT LUCIUS MAINTAINED THAT THE LINK IS MORE SYMBOLIC.

BY TRIGGERING THE MECHANISM HIDDEN AT THE CENTER OF THE HANDLE, THE CROSS CAPTURES THE WORDS AND THE IMAGE OF THE PERSON HOLDING IT.
AND BY REVERSING THE PROCESS, THE CROSS STORES THEM.
I CAN'T UNDERSTAND HOW SUCH A PHENOMENON IS POSSIBLE. THIS IS ABSOLUTELY ASTONISHING!
YES. BUT, ALAS, THE KNOWLEDGE THAT WOULD EXPLAIN THE INNER WORKINGS OF THIS OBJECT HAS BEEN LOST.
A SCIENCE CAPABLE OF PRODUCING SUCH A MIRACLE COULD ONLY BE THE WORK OF THE GODS.
THE GODS DO NOT EXPLAIN EVERYTHING, VALERIA. IT APPEARS THERE WAS A CIVILIZATION WHICH PRECEDED OURS. A GLITTERING CIVILIZATION, ITS TECHNOLOGIES FAR ADVANCED BEYOND OUR UNDERSTANDING. NO TRACE OF IT EXISTS TODAY—
SAVE SOME OBJECTS.
DID LUCIUS TELL YOU WHAT PURPOSE HE ANTICIPATED FOR THE ANKH?
NO. HE SHOWED ME HOW TO USE IT, BUT HE DIED BEFORE TELLING ME WHY HE NEEDED IT.
AND YOU THINK THAT HE LEFT A MESSAGE INTENDED FOR YOU?
I HOPE SO! BECAUSE IF HE DIDN'T, MY ENTIRE MISSION WILL HAVE BEEN IN VAIN!
KLIKK!
26

RRRRR!
TKK
AQUILUS... KZZT... I DON'T KNOW IF THIS OBJECT IS FUNCTIONING AS IT SHOULD... KZZT...
KZZT... I AM ALSO UNAWARE IF THIS MESSAGE WILL REACH YOU... KZZT... KNOW, HOWEVER, THAT VULTUR HAS BETRAYED US.... HIS FRIENDSHIP IS A RUSE... KZZT... HE ONLY CAME HERE TO STEAL THE ANKH... I HEAR HIM COMING, NO DOUBT SO HE CAN KILL ME...
I DO NOT HAVE MUCH TIME... OUR TASK, AQUILUS, CONCERNS THE LIBERALIS CIRCULUM... KZZT... A FACTION THAT OUR FAMILY HAS BEEN A PART OF FOR GENERATIONS...
KZZT... ONE OF THE FOUNDERS OF THE CIRCLE HAS DIED... KZZT... TAKING IMPORTANT INFORMATION WITH HIM: THE LOCATION OF AN OBJECT!
27

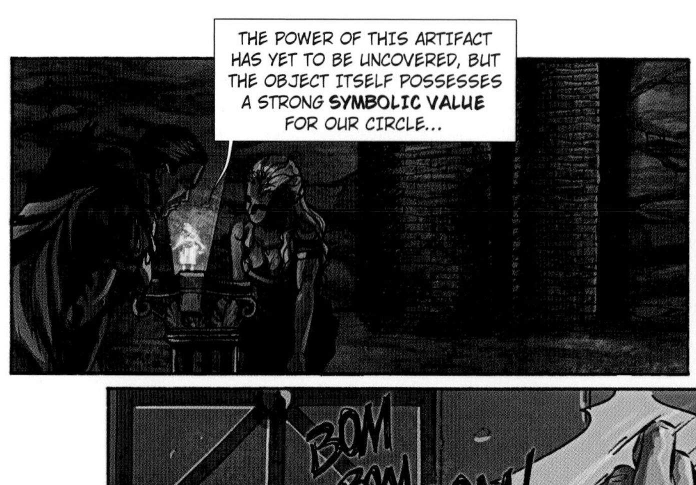
THE POWER OF THIS ARTIFACT HAS YET TO BE UNCOVERED, BUT THE OBJECT ITSELF POSSESSES A STRONG **SYMBOLIC VALUE** FOR OUR CIRCLE...

ONE OF THESE FOUNDERS... **LUGOS**--

BOM BOM BOM!

BOM BOM BOM!
?!

OPEN UP!
ALL RIGHT, ALL RIGHT!

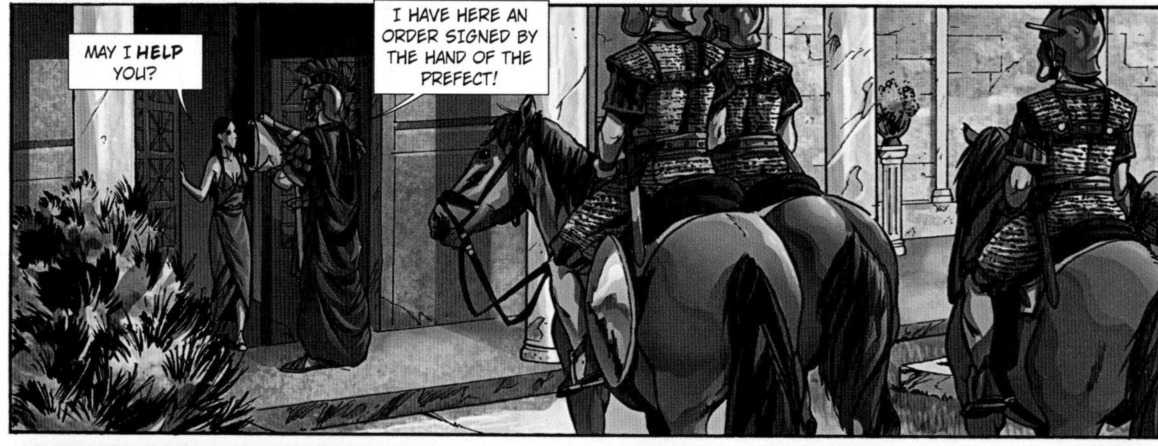
MAY I **HELP** YOU?
I HAVE HERE AN ORDER SIGNED BY THE HAND OF THE PREFECT!

WARN YOUR MASTER THAT WE ARE COMING TO ARREST HIM!
ARREST HIM? BUT... BUT WHY?

28.

AQUILUS HASN'T DONE ANYTHING **WRONG**--
THAT IS NOT FOR YOU TO JUDGE! OUT OF THE WAY!

WHERE IS HE?
AT THE BACK... IN THE CRYPT.

LEAD US THERE!

I AM SORRY, MASTER.
WHO GAVE YOU **PERMISSION** TO ENTER MY HOME?
AQUILUS, SON OF LUCIUS--BY THE ORDER OF ROME, YOU ARE UNDER ARREST! GIVE YOURSELF UP!

I ***WILL*** GIVE MYSELF UP WHEN YOU TELL ME **WHAT** I AM ACCUSED OF!

YOU ASSASSINATED **FAUSTINUS**, THE BISHOP OF LUGDUNUM!

EVERY MEMBER OF HIS HOUSE STAFF SAW YOU COMMIT THIS CRIME AND THEY ARE PREPARED TO **TESTIFY** AGAINST YOU.
I DO NOT DENY COMMITTING THIS CRIME. THAT **PIG** WAS A TRAITOR! BUT IF YOU WANT TO ARREST ME, YOU WILL HAVE TO COME AND **FIND ME** FIRST!
GRAB HOLD OF HIM!
SCHOCK!
SCHOCK!
TNK!
OW!
PICK HIM UP AND TIE HIM.

31

[1]ROANNE, LOIR, FRANCE.

SEVERAL HOURS LATER, FAR FROM LUGDUNUM.
WHY ARE YOU TAKING US TO RODUMNA?
OUR ORDERS ARE TO ESCORT YOU THERE, GAUL, NOT TO MAKE CONVERSATION!
YOU'VE CAPTURED US AND TIED US UP! AT LEAST HAVE THE DECENCY TO INFORM US OF THE PURPOSE OF OUR JOURNEY!
BECAUSE OF THE THREAT POSED BY THE ALEMANNI, SEVERAL HIGH DIGNITARIES HAVE LEFT LUGDUNUM AND FOUND REFUGE IN RODUMNA.
YOU WILL BE TRIED BY THEM THERE.

TRIED?
YES! AND WE WILL ALSO HAND OVER THE STRANGE OBJECT WE FOUND IN THE CELLAR OF YOUR VILLA.

I AM SURE THAT THEY WILL VERY INTERESTED.

EUGH!

TAKE COVER! WE'RE BEING ATTACKED!
KILL THE PRISONERS! KILL THEM!

AARGH

DIE, YOU ASSASSIN DOG!

AAAHHH!

AAAHHH!

WHAT'S HAPPENING?!
AQUILUS IS DEAD!
NOOOOOO!!

33

THE VIOLENT SHOCK HAS ECHOED AS FAR BACK AS DESMOND'S CEREBRAL CORTEX!
I'VE DISCONNECTED EVERYTHING!
MY GOD...
DESMOND? HOW ARE YOU FEELING?
I... I'M OKAY...
THE DEATH OF YOUR ANCESTRAL SUBJECT SEEMS TO HAVE AUTOMATICALLY SEVERED THE CONNECTION BETWEEN THE PAST AND THE PRESENT.
THAT'S WHAT WAS MEANT TO HAPPEN. GUYS, I DON'T KNOW HOW TO TELL YOU THIS. I... I THINK THAT VALERIA IS PREGNANT.
SHE'S PREGNANT?
SHE HAS TO BE! THE DATA IS SPIKING--IT'S ALL OVER THE PLACE. THERE'S NO OTHER EXPLANATION.
I WANT TO CARRY ON WITH THIS SESSION, LUCY. RECONNECT ME TO THE ANIMUS! NOW--
OUT OF THE QUESTION! YOU HAVE TO REST, DESMOND!
AFTER WHAT JUST HAPPENED, I NEED TO KNOW THAT VALERIA IS OKAY!
AQUILUS IS DEAD, LUCY! HE WAS KILLED WITHOUT HONOR, ON THE EDGE OF A COUNTRY ROAD, HIS HANDS TIED TOGETHER. THEY DENIED HIM THE RIGHT TO DEFEND HIS LIFE AND DIE WITH DIGNITY.
MY ANCESTOR WAS KILLED LIKE AN ANIMAL! BUT I REFUSE TO BELIEVE THAT HE WAS KILLED FOR NOTHING! I WANT TO KNOW! SEND ME BACK IN THERE!
OKAY, OKAY. IF THAT'S WHAT YOU WANT.
34

AQUILUS! NO!
NOOO!
NOOOOOOOOO!!
AQUILUS!
CRRAA!
CRAAAA!
AQUILUS...
THEY KILLED HIM! THEY KILLED HIM!
CRAAAA!
CRAA!

35

HOUU
HOU HOUUU
LET'S STOP AWHILE. I DON'T THINK ANYONE IS FOLLOWING US AND YOU ARE EXHAUSTED.
36

HOW DID YOU KNOW WHERE WE WERE?
I WAS INFORMED OF YOUR ARREST BY CHANCE.
I HURRIED TO THE VILLA, BUT ARRIVED TOO LATE. THE SOLDIERS HAD ALREADY TAKEN YOU. IT WAS YOUR HOUSEMAID WHO TOLD ME THAT YOU WERE BEING CARTED TO RODUMNA TO BE TRIED THERE. I GALLOPED ALL THE WAY...BECAUSE I KNEW THAT THE PREFECT PLANNED TO KILL YOU ALONG THE WAY.
JUST BEFORE THE SOLDIERS INVADED OUR HOME, AQUILUS REVEALED THE MYSTERY BEHIND THIS STRANGE OBJECT.
THE ANKH. IT WAS I THAT GAVE IT TO HIM. DO YOU KNOW IF HE WAS ABLE TO USE IT?
YES... I WAS THERE...
AN IMAGE OF LUCIUS APPEARED. HE MENTIONED THAT SOMEONE WAS CARRYING THE KNOWLEDGE AS TO THE WHEREABOUTS OF A VERY IMPORTANT OBJECT.
DO YOU REMEMBER THE NAME OF THIS PERSON?
I... I THINK IT WAS LUGOS...
AND THE LOCATION?
NO, NO. I'M SORRY.
RIGHT, THEN WE MUST RETRACE YOUR FOOTSTEPS. DO YOU KNOW HOW TO USE THE CROSS?
37

FATE IS TRYING DESPERATELY TO WORK AGAINST US! THE DEATHS OF LUCIUS AND AQUILUS ARE A TERRIBLE BLOW TO THE LIBERALIS CIRCULUM.
YOUR CIRCLE IS NOT AT THE CENTER OF THE WORLD, ACCIPITER! ME, I'VE LOST A FATHER-IN-LAW AND A HUSBAND! EVERYTHING I ONCE LOVED HAS GONE.
FORGIVE ME, VALERIA. ANGER HAS RENDERED ME BLIND TO YOUR GRIEF.
WHAT ARE YOU GOING TO DO NOW? RETURNING TO LUGDUNUM IS OUT OF THE QUESTION. YOU WOULD BE HUNTED AND IMPRISONED!
I'M GOING TO TRY MY LUCK ON THE ITALIAN COAST. A COUSIN OF AQUILUS LIVES IN MONTERIGGIONI. SHE WILL BE ABLE TO ACCOMMODATE ME FOR A FEW MONTHS, ENOUGH TIME TO DELIVER MY BABY.
TAKE THIS! TAKE THIS DAMNED OBJECT! I NO LONGER WANT IT!
I AM OUT IN THE COUNTRY. I COULD BE KILLED AT ANY INSTANT! I DON'T WANT TO RISK THE ANKH FALLING INTO THE HANDS OF OUR ENEMIES.
WHAT CAN WE DO ABOUT IT?
ONCE YOU REACH MONTERIGGIONI, YOU MUST ERECT AN ALTAR TO THE MEMORY OF AQUILUS, AND PLACE THE CROSS WITHIN IT. UNTIL I FIND ANOTHER WAY TO DISCOVER THE LOCATION OF THE OBJECT THAT LUCIUS SPOKE OF, THE ANKH WILL BE SAFEST THERE.
I WILL DO AS YOU WISH...
WATCHED
QUILUS. I
NK I CAN DO
AT HE DID.
-SIGH- I FEAR THAT IT WILL BE USELESS. WE LISTENED TO LUCIUS' MESSAGE TO THE END. HE DIDN'T OFFER ANY DETAILS ABOUT A POSSIBLE LOCATION. VULTUR KILLED HIM BEFORE HE COULD DO SO!

DESMOND? ARE YOU ALL RIGHT?
I... I KNOW WHERE TO FIND THE ANKH!
AQUILUS IS ENSHRINED HERE, IN MONTERIGGIONI. HIS WIFE, VALERIA, PLACED THE CROSS IN THIS ALTAR.
IT DOESN'T MAKE SENSE, DESMOND!
REBECCA SIFTED THROUGH THE VILLA'S ARCHIVES. IT'S NOT AQUILUS WHO'S CONSECRATED HERE, IT'S LUGOS!
LOOK!
THIS SYMBOL DOESN'T REPRESENT AN EAGLE. IT'S A RAVEN!
IT WOULD HAVE BEEN DISRESPECTFUL TO THE MEMORY OF THESE TWO MEN TO PLACE THEM SIDE BY SIDE. AQUILUS' ALTAR HAS PROBABLY BEEN BURNT TO THE GROUND.
OKAY, FINE--SO MAYBE YOU'RE RIGHT. BUT VALERIA DIDN'T GET RID OF THE ANKH. SHE MIGHT HAVE HIDDEN IT HERE!

39

THERE MUST BE SOME SORT OF **HIDING PLACE**.
IT'S NOT SEALED.
CRRR
THIS STONE, MAYBE?
THERE'S THE ANKH!
IT'S **STILL** INTACT, EVEN AFTER ALL THIS TIME.
IT'S ONE OF A GROUP OF ARTIFACTS INTRICATELY CRAFTED BY THE ARTISANS OF A CIVILIZATION THAT HAS ALL BUT DISAPPEARED. THEY CREATED THESE OBJECTS TO DEEPEN THEIR KNOWELDGE OF HIDDEN WORLDS! IT'S INDESTRUCTIBLE!
ACCIPITER MADE AN ERROR IN JUDGMENT. HE WOULD HAVE HAD TO FOLLOW HIS INSTINCTS TO MAKE THE CROSS WORK.
WHY DIDN'T HE DO IT?
I DON'T KNOW. MAYBE, IN THE CONFUSION, HE THOUGHT THAT IT ONLY CONTAINED **LUCIUS'** MESSAGE. WHAT VALERIA SAID WAS ALONG THOSE LINES--ACCIPITER DIDN'T HAVE REASON TO DOUBT HER.
AND IF THAT **WAS** THE CASE? IF THE CROSS DIDN'T CONTAIN ANY **OTHER** 'RECORDING'?
THEN **NOBODY** WILL BE ABLE TO COMPLETE AQUILUS' MISSION! EVER.
40

KLIKK!
LOOK, LUCY! THERE'S A FIGURE APPEARING!
KZZT... MY NAME IS LUGOS... KZZT...

41

...KZZT... ONE OF THE FOUNDERS OF LIBERALIS CIRCULUM... KZZT...
OUR SHIP WAS DESTROYED BY A TERRIBLE STORM IN THE MIDDLE OF THE MARE INTERNUM... AN ENORMOUS WATERWAY OPENED BEFORE US... KZZT...
ALAS, WE ARE TOO FAR FROM THE COAST TO HOPE TO SURVIVE BY SWIMMING... KZZT... THE BOAT IS SINKING. MY FINAL MOMENTS ARE APPROACHING...
MY MISSION HAS FAILED... THE OBJECT WE HAD TO RETRIEVE IS LOST FOREVER... KZZT...

MARE INTERNUM...
IN LATIN, THAT MEANS 'THE INTERNAL SEA'...
OKAY--SO WHAT?

THAT'S WHAT THE ROMANS CALLED THE MEDITERRANEAN. THEY ALSO USED TO CALL IT THE 'MARE NOSTRUM'*.

WAIT. LET ME GET THIS STRAIGHT. LUGOS' ARTIFACT IS ON BOARD A WRECKAGE WHICH HAS BEEN ROTTING AWAY AT THE BOTTOM OF THE MEDITERRANEAN FOR ALMOST TWO THOUSAND YEARS?

AND THAT SERIOUSLY LIMITS OUR CHANCES OF EVER GETTING OUR HANDS ON IT!
THAT DEPENDS. BACK THEN, IT PROBABLY SEEMED LIKE AN UNACHIEVABLE TASK. TODAY, TECHNOLOGY HAS EVOLVED. WE CAN SURVEY THE SEA FLOOR AND FISH OUT THE SUNKEN TREASURE FROM BELOW.
LET'S NOT GET CARRIED AWAY. WE HAVE TO PRESENT OUR FINDINGS TO OTHER TEAMS AND MAKE A JOINT DECISION.

ALL THAT WORK, FOR THIS? WHAT A WASTE!
I UNDERSTAND YOUR DISAPPOINTMENT, DESMOND. BUT I'M AFRAID THIS DECISION IS NOT OURS TO MAKE.

BEEEP BEEP

*'OUR SEA'.

YEAH?
DESMOND MILES?
THAT'S ME. WHO'S ASKING?
MY NAME IS **STELLA CROW**. YOU DON'T KNOW ME. ASK LUCY FOR FILE NUMBER 24. GIVE IT TO THE PERSON WHO TURNS UP TO COLLECT IT.
HANG ON. **FILE 24**? WHAT ARE YOU **TALKING** ABOUT? I DON'T UNDERSTAND...
GOODBYE, **MR MILES**.

SHE HUNG UP. WHAT KIND OF **MESS** AM I GETTING MIXED UP IN **NOW**?

LUCY, DO YOU KNOW ANYTHING ABOUT 'FILE 24'?
YES. IT WAS DELIVERED TO US BY MESSENGER TWO DAYS AGO.

UMMM--I SHOULD WAIT FOR STELLA TO CALL BEFORE I GIVE IT TO YOU--
WHAT IS IT?

I DON'T KNOW. I HAVEN'T OPENED IT.

IT'S PROBABLY THE DETAILS FOR YOUR NEW **MISSION**, DESMOND.

WHO'S STELLA CROW?

SHE'S A MEMBER OF THE **ORDER OF ASSASSINS**, LIKE YOU, DESMOND.
ACCORDING TO HER GENEALOGY, SHE'S A **DESCENDANT** OF **LUGOS**.

THERE'S SOMEONE AT THE DOOR.

I THINK IT'S JONATHAN HAWK.
I'LL GET THE DOOR.

HAWK? WE WEREN'T XPECTING HIM. WHAT'S **HE** DOING HERE?
ACCORDING TO CROW, I HAVE TO HAND THIS FILE OVER TO HIM.

THE PLANS MUST HAVE CHANGED. SURELY HAWK'S HERE TO **REPLACE** DESMOND!

GOT IT IN ONE, MR HASTINGS. THE MISSION PARAMETERS HAVE BEEN **RECONFIGURED**. I'VE BEEN ASSIGNED TO **THIS** TEAM.

DESMOND, THIS IS JONATHAN HAWK.
PLEASURE.
BACK AT YA.

I'VE HEARD SO MUCH ABOUT YOU, MR MILES.
I WISH I COULD SAY THE SAME ABOUT YOU, JONATHAN.

ALTHOUGH--I 'VE GOT THE **STRANGEST** FEELING I'VE SEEN YOU SOMEWHERE BEFORE.

HEH, YOU COULD SAY THAT. AS A MATTER OF FACT, WE **HAVE** ALREADY MET. I AM A **DESCENDANT** OF ACCIPITER.

SO--WE'RE DISTANT COUSINS?
THEN, I GUESS **THIS** BELONGS TO YOU.
THANKS.
HMMM. WELL, RIGHT NOW, I'M NOT ENTIRELY SURE WHAT THE **MISSION** INVOLVES--
SO, WHAT HAVE I MANAGED TO GET AWAY FROM?

BUT I DO HAVE **SOME** IDEA OF WHERE WE MIGHT BE GOING...
END OF BOOK THREE.